D0536835

SECRET
OF THE
SLEEPLESS
WHALES
...AND MORE!

BY ANA MARÍA RODRÍGUEZ

★ ANIMAL
SECRETS
REVEALED! ★

Author Ana María Rodríguez would like to express immense gratitude to all of the scientists who have contributed to the *Animal Secrets Revealed!* series. Their photos and comments have been invaluable for the creation of these books.

Library of Congress Cataloging-in-Publication Data

Rodríguez, Ana María, 1958—
  Secret of the sleepless whales— and more! / Ana María Rodríguez.
     p. cm. — (Animal secrets revealed!)
  Summary: "Explains how and why whales live without much sleep and details other strange abilities of different types of animals"—Provided by publisher.
  Includes bibliographical references and index.
  ISBN-13: 978-0-7660-2957-6
  ISBN-10: 0-7660-2957-3
  1. Marine mammals—Juvenile literature. 2. Marine mammals—Research—Juvenile literature. I. Title.
  QL713.2.R63 2009
  599.5—dc22

                                    2007039479

Printed in the United States of America

10 9 8 7 6 5 4 3 2

To Our Readers: We have done our best to make sure all Internet addresses in this book were active and appropriate when we went to press. However, the author and the publisher have no control over and assume no liability for the material available on those Internet sites or on other Web sites they may link to. Any comments or suggestions can be sent by e-mail to comments@enslow.com or to the address on the back cover.

☘ Enslow Publishers, Inc., is committed to printing our books on recycled paper. The paper in every book contains 10% to 30% post-consumer waste (PCW). The cover board on the outside of each book contains 100% PCW. Our goal is to do our part to help young people and the environment too!

Illustration Credits: Donald LeRoi/National Oceanic & Atmospheric Administration (NOAA) Southwest Fisheries Science Center/ National Science Foundation (NSF)-US. Antarctic Program, p. 21; Guido Dehnhardt/Marine Science Center Germany, pp. 24, 25, 26, 28; Hawaii Institute of Marine Biology/ University of Hawaii on Coconut Island, p. 32; Hiroya Minakuchi/Minden Pictures, p. 33; Janet Mann, p. 31; Kevin McDonnell/University of California Santa Cruz, p. 6; National Science Foundation-US. Antarctic Program/ Joe Stanford, p. 20; Norbert Wu/Minden Pictures, p. 11; Opher Ganel/University of Maryland/ National Science Foundation (NSF), p. 37; Randall W. Davis/ Texas A&M University/ funding from the National Science Foundation (NSF), Division of Polar Programs, pp. 38, 39, 41; Sea World San Diego, copyright 2006, p. 18; Terrie Williams/ University of California Santa Cruz, p. 9.

Cover Illustration: © SeaPics.com.

★ CONTENTS ★

★

ENTER THE WORLD OF ANIMAL SECRETS!

Aquatic mammals do amazing things! Tag along with scientists to discover how Popolo the dolphin is able to dive for long periods of time. Other dolphins like Dodger reveal the secret strategy they use to avoid dangerous encounters with prey. Killer whale Kasatka and her calf Nakai showed scientists what they "do not do" to survive the first weeks after the baby is born. Ally the Weddell seal revealed her unexpected hunting tactic, and Henry the harbor seal has shown scientists why murky, dark waters are no problem for him when it is time to find a meal. Join the scientists and their animal partners in an amazing adventure!

1
DIVING DOLPHIN'S SECRET

Hold your breath! Get set, dive! How deep can you swim before you run out of air? Sometimes not even to the bottom of the diving pool. If you have not practiced, even getting to the bottom of the pool can be a challenge. Swimming during diving demands a lot of energy from our bodies. It also demands a lot from mammals that live in the water, such as dolphins, seals, and whales.

Scientists have calculated how much oxygen a dolphin would need to swim as deep as two hundred meters (656 feet) and come back to the surface. And according to what they found, dolphins should not have enough oxygen for the round trip![1] But obviously they do, so what is their secret?

Popolo the dolphin carries equipment on its back. The camera and other instruments are attached with a non-slip belt hooked into the dolphin's fin.

Scientists had to find a way to record the dolphins' behavior while they were performing deep dives. They decided to attach a camera to the dolphin's back to film its behavior underwater.[2] This idea turned out to be a challenge.

Nonstick Skin

For their first experiments, Dr. Terrie Williams and her team at the University of California in Santa Cruz decided to partner up with Popolo. He is a trained dolphin of the Navy. Working with Popolo would be easier than working with a wild dolphin because Popolo is used to interacting with people. He is friendly and cooperative.[3]

Popolo and a scientist diver went underwater together. The diver began attaching the recording equipment on Popolo when, surprise! The dolphin's skin was so slippery that the equipment kept falling off. "One of the amazing things about dolphin and whale skin is that nothing sticks to it," said Dr. Williams.

"These animals could never wear a bandage if they got cut because it would just fall off."[4] Popolo's nonstick skin made it very tricky when the scientist tried to attach the cameras on the dolphin's back.

Saddle Up and Suction

Dr. Williams and her team tried different ways to attach the camera on Popolo. First, they tried a custom-made saddle that fitted over the dorsal fin (this is the fin on the dolphin's back that shows up on the water when dolphins swim close to the surface). The saddle was fastened around the dolphin's belly with a thin strap. This worked fine.[5]

The scientists also used a special wet suit for Popolo that had a suction backing. The large suction cup held the camera and other equipment in place as the dolphin swam and dove. Popolo did not seem to be bothered by it.

THE BIG PICTURE

Aquatic mammals have many characteristics that contribute to their amazing diving abilities:

★ They have more blood than terrestrial mammals do. For example, the amount of blood an elephant seal has is about 12 percent of its body weight, while the amount of blood people have is about 7 percent of their body weight.

★ The blood of aquatic mammals stores more oxygen than human blood. For example, a harbor seal stores twice as much oxygen in one hundred milliliters (0.42 cup) of blood than a person does in the same volume.

Blood carries the much needed oxygen to the whole body. The more blood an animal has and the more oxygen that blood carries, the higher the supply of precious oxygen the animal can count on for its activities.[6]

**DOLPHIN SECRET:
COLLAPSIBLE LUNGS**

A diving scientist attaches the equipment on Popolo's body.

Popolo even modeled the equipment he wore for the other dolphins in the area!

Popolo Reveals the Secret

To be able to "see" what Popolo was seeing and where he was heading during his dives, the scientists placed the camera pointing toward Popolo's head. Other times, the scientists turned the "head-cam" into a "rear end-cam." This allowed the camera to film Popolo's tail so that the scientists could determine the frequency, or the number of times, he stroked his tail when he dived. About three minutes passed from the time Popolo dived to the time he came back to the surface to breathe.[7] Dr. Williams and her team discovered that during deep dives, Popolo did not swim or move his tail up and down all the time, like you would kick your feet while diving. He just let himself sink sometimes.[8] The scientists wondered, why did Popolo stop moving his tail and just let himself glide? It turned out that the pressure of the water above Popolo had a lot to do with his amazing behavior.

Sink and Save

When Popolo reached a depth of about eighty meters (around two hundred sixty feet), the pressure of the water above him compressed, or squeezed, his lungs. This caused the lungs to slowly collapse,[9] like if you applied pressure on a small air-filled balloon with your hands until it became almost

When the pressure of the water above the dolphins makes their lungs collapse, they simply stop swimming and sink.

flat (but not so hard that it popped).

When Popolo's lungs naturally collapsed, he was not hurt. He floated less and sank easily. Pretend that you were diving holding an air-filled balloon in your arms. If you could apply enough pressure on it so it would become very flat without popping, then it would be easier for you to dive deeper.

As Popolo swam back to the surface, there was less and less water above him, so the water pressure on his lungs was also reduced. Then, his lungs slowly expanded again before he reached the surface.[10] It would be like if you stopped squeezing or released the pressure on your imaginary balloon as you went back to the surface. The balloon would then return to its original volume and you would float back up to the surface.

The diving dolphin's secret was out. Dolphins can dive longer because they save oxygen on their way down. They

THE DEEPEST MAMMAL DIVERS

Whales win first place as the deepest mammal divers known. Some sperm whales have been recorded to dive to two thousand meters (6,562 feet) for about sixty minutes,[11] and Cuvier's beaked whales are able to dive to about nineteen hundred meters (6,234 feet) for eighty-five minutes.[12] These diving depths are larger than the world's tallest building—Toronto's CN Tower in Canada. This tower is 553.3 meters tall (1,815.3 feet). The depth the whales can dive is large enough to fit about three and a half Toronto's CN Towers one on top of each other.

★ Dr. Williams and other scientists have discovered that Weddell seals, elephant seals, and deep-diving whales also experience lung collapse during deep dives and practice the "sink and save" strategy.

save oxygen because they stop swimming and let themselves sink. They take advantage of their natural lung collapse that makes it easier for them to go down. Dolphins just go with the flow, saving the costly effort of swimming to chase fish underwater and even avoid predators like sharks before swimming back up to take a much needed breath.

Try It Yourself: Feel the Pressure

The deeper the dive, the higher the pressure. You have probably felt it. Pressure can make your ears ache when you dive in a pool or the ocean. For every 10 meters (32.8 feet) a diver descends, the body receives an additional 1.03 kilograms per square centimeter (14.7 pounds per square inch) of pressure.

In this experiment you will apply pressure to a submerged eyedropper with a "lung" (an air bubble inside) and see how the pressure affects the eyedropper's ability to float.

Materials
★ 500-milliliter (16.9-ounce) transparent soft plastic water bottle with cap (as soft as the 2-liter bottles). Remove the label.
★ water
★ transparent eyedropper

Procedure
1 Fill the 500-milliliter plastic bottle to the top with water.

2 Fill the eyedropper about three-quarters with water, leaving a bubble inside.

3 Place the eyedropper inside the bottle, rubber on top. Let it bob.

4 Make sure the water in the bottle is up to the rim and close the bottle tightly with the cap.

5 Squeeze the middle of the bottle tightly with your hands. What happens to the eyedropper?

Tips: You may have to try different sizes of bubbles inside the eyedropper by filling it with more or less water until you find the bubble size that allows you to control how deep the eye-dropper dives.

Observe and Answer

1 What happens to the eyedropper when you squeeze the bottle?

2 What happens to the bubble inside the eyedropper (the "lung") when you squeeze the bottle?

3 What happens to the eyedropper and the bubble inside it when you release the squeeze in the bottle?

Like dolphins' lungs, human lungs also get squeezed when free divers dive deep. When a free diver (one with no diving equipment) reaches a depth of 100 meters (328.1 feet), his lung capacity is 0.37 liters (1.56 cups). Back on the surface, the average lung capacity is 5.5 liters (23.2 cups). At 100 meters (328.1 feet) deep, the water pressure above the free diver squeezes his lungs to less than a tenth of their capacity at the surface, and the diver sinks effortlessly.

2
SLEEPLESS IN THE OCEAN

Scientists thought that newborn baby mammals needed to sleep a lot for their brains and body to grow and develop. However, all the animals that had been studied so far were terrestrial, or living on land. Nobody had studied aquatic mammals before.

Dr. Jerry Siegel and his colleagues from the Center for Sleep Research at the University of California in Los Angeles decided to take a look at the sleeping habits of baby orcas (killer whales) and dolphins. Do they sleep as much as baby mammals that live on land? The American scientists teamed up with Russian scientist Oleg Lyamin. Dr. Lyamin studied killer whales at SeaWorld San Diego and dolphins in Russian research stations in the Black Sea region.

SLEEP FACTS

How much an animal sleeps mostly depends on its body size. In general, the larger the animal, the less sleep it requires. Scientists think that one of the functions of sleep is to repair damage to brain cells. Smaller animals have higher metabolic rates (their bodies work faster—for example, their hearts beat faster than larger animals' hearts). Higher metabolic rates lead to more injuries to cells in the body, so they may require more sleep time to repair them.

This table shows how many hours (h) different adult animals sleep in a twenty-four-hour period.[1]

Opossum	Ferret	Cat	Dog	Human	Elephant
18 h	14.4 h	12.5 h	10.1 h	8 h	3 h

Sleeping in the Water

First, the scientists observed how (and how much) adult orcas and dolphins sleep. How do you know when an orca or a dolphin is sleeping? These animals do not have a long good night's sleep like people do. Orcas and dolphins usually sleep floating motionless at the surface of the water for up to forty minutes at a time. Sometimes orcas also sleep by resting still at the bottom of the pool for up to seven minutes at a time. Dolphins, however, may also sleep while they are swimming.[2] Once the scientists knew how much adult orcas and dolphins sleep, they were ready to compare their sleeping habits with those of their newborn babies. They just needed a few new babies to be born to observe their sleeping behavior during their first weeks after birth.

> **Meet the Scientists:** *Dr. Jerry Siegel and Dr. Oleg Lyamin are marine biologists interested in studying how aquatic animals sleep.*

Watching Babies "Sleep"

Dr. Siegel and his group were very excited when they found out that Kasatka, an orca living at SeaWorld San Diego, had given birth to a baby named Nakai. In Russia's Dolphinarium, a place similar to SeaWorld in America, four dolphins were about to give birth. These were perfect opportunities for the American and Russian scientists to do their experiments, so they headed to SeaWorld and the Dolphinarium to watch the babies sleep.

Kasatka and her calf, Nakai, swim in their giant pool at SeaWorld San Diego, where Nakai was born. Neither mom nor calf slept for the first four weeks after Nakai's birth.

For about four weeks after birth, the baby dolphins and baby orcas swam all the time. They did not rest on the surface or at the bottom of the pool as adults do when they sleep. This meant that the babies did not seem to sleep and their mothers did not sleep much either. The mothers sometimes stayed still at the surface of the pool while the babies surfaced to breathe, which they did very often, every three to thirty seconds. The babies constantly swam around and under their mothers producing high-pitched sounds. They also followed their mothers wherever they went around the pool.[3]

One Eye Shut

The scientists also looked at the animals' eyes. Adult dolphins and orcas seem to sleep with half of their brain at one time. It is true. Scientists have studied these

Science Tongue Twister: *The scientific name of Kasatka the orca is* Orcinus orca.

animals' brains and know that when the right hemisphere, or right side of the brain, has brain waves that occur during sleep, the dolphin's left eye is closed. The opposite is also true. If the left hemisphere of the brain has brain waves that occur during sleep, then the animal's right eye will be closed and the left eye open.[4]

When the scientists watched the babies and their mothers come to the surface to breathe, they looked at their eyes to see if they were open or closed. They also watched the twenty-four-hour videos to confirm that this happened day and night. Neither the moms nor the babies shut one eye during the first four weeks after birth. They were definitely awake, with both eyes open when they surfaced.[5]

This surprising behavior lasted about one month. After three to four weeks, both babies and their mothers began to close their eyes and sleep for longer and longer periods of time until they slept like adults do. When three-month-old baby dolphins sleep, they close one eye at a time and keep the open eye always directed toward their mother. They want to know where mom is all the time!

Killer whales surface near Ross Island, Antarctica. Although called "whales," they are more related to dolphins.

Sleepless to Survive

Scientists are still puzzled about how baby dolphins and baby orcas and their mothers stay awake for so long. Without long periods of sleep, rats would die. When people have their sleep interrupted, they are less able to concentrate on tasks and make more mistakes.[6]

Scientists think that one of the reasons baby dolphins and orcas do not go to sleep during the first four weeks after birth is to stay on the move to avoid predators. Another reason may have to do with the need to stay warm. As opposed to baby land mammals, baby water mammals do not have a cozy, safe, warm place to curl up and go to sleep. They swim

Three adult killer whales and a calf swim in McMurdo Sound, Antarctica. Some can grow to huge dimensions reaching nearly 10 meters long (33 feet), which is almost as long as an average school bus (about 12 meters or 40 feet).

in ice-cold water all the time. So scientists think that baby dolphins and orcas may stay awake to keep moving. Swimming produces body heat that helps to maintain warmth in their bodies while they grow a thick layer of fat under their skin called blubber. Blubber acts like an insulator—like a big thick winter jacket—that keeps them warm in ice-cold water.[7] Mom, in the meantime, may have to stay awake to keep an eye on the baby to make sure it eats and stays out of trouble.

3
HUNGRY SEALS
DO THE TWIST

enry the seal is no ordinary harbor
seal. His name has appeared in one
of the top-ranking science journals
most scientists read every week.
Henry's name is in the science
journal because he has helped German scientists
uncover one of the best well-kept seal secrets.
How do harbor seals find their food in the dark if
they cannot see? It turned out that the answer was
right on the seal's face.

In the wild, harbor seals like Henry usually
hunt for their meals—fish, shrimp, and squid—in
places where they cannot see very well.
Sometimes they hunt at night. Other times they
hunt in deep water where light does not reach.
Many times, harbor seals hunt in murky water
where they cannot see very well either. But even

though they cannot "see" their prey, seals are successful hunters. Scientists have even seen blind seals in the wild that look well fed, which means they are capable of catching their meals.[1] How do they find and catch a moving fish without seeing it?

Feeling the Water Move

Unlike dolphins, which can also hunt in dark waters, seals do not use echolocation or a sonar system to find their prey using sound. Other aquatic animals, like some fish, have a different system called "lateral line" that senses ripples of water like those left by swimming fish. However, scientists do not know yet if fish are capable of following the ripples for tracking their prey.[2]

> *Science Tongue Twister:*
> **The scientific name of Henry the harbor seal is Phoca vitulina**

Scientists call this a "hydrodynamic trail." Hydrodynamic means "movement (dynamic) of liquids (hydro)." Dr. Guido Dehnhardt and his colleagues at the University of Bochum in Germany decided to find out if harbor seals had a "ripple-detecting system" and if they used it to hunt in the dark.

Look Mom, No Flippers!

Scientists already knew a few things about seals from experiments they had done.

> **Meet the Scientists:**
> *Dr. Guido Dehnhardt and his colleagues are marine biologists interested in learning how seals use their senses in the water.*

23

Henry the seal feels a lollipop using his ultra-sensitive whiskers.

For example, they knew that harbor seals can use their whiskers to determine the size of objects as well as monkeys use their hands. Harbor seals can tell apart discs of different sizes by just touching them with their whiskers.[3]

This is possible because each of the forty-four whiskers—scientists call them *vibrissae*—on each side of the seal's snout is connected to the brain by about thirteen hundred nerve fibers. This is about ten times more connections than those present in other animals with whiskers like rats and cats. The more connections between the whiskers and the brain, the more the brain knows about what the seal is touching. Having whiskers that are ten times more sensitive comes in "handy" for seals since their limbs have evolved into flippers. Flippers are good for swimming, but they are not as good as hands for touching.[4]

If harbor seal whiskers are very sensitive to touch, maybe they can feel tiny ripples in the water. Here is where Henry the seal helped scientists. Henry became a partner of

Henry, blindfolded and wearing headphones, explores the researcher's hand using his whiskers.

Dr. Dehnhardt and his group and showed them how harbor seals hunt in the dark.

Follow that Sub!

Henry the seal and Dr. Dehnhardt and his team worked at the Marine Science Center at Zoo Cologne in Germany. The station has a pool in which the scientists began their experiments by teaching Henry to follow a self-propelled toy submarine.

The submarine had a head start, leaving a track of ripples behind it. After about four seconds, the submarine's engine turned off and Henry was signaled to start the search.

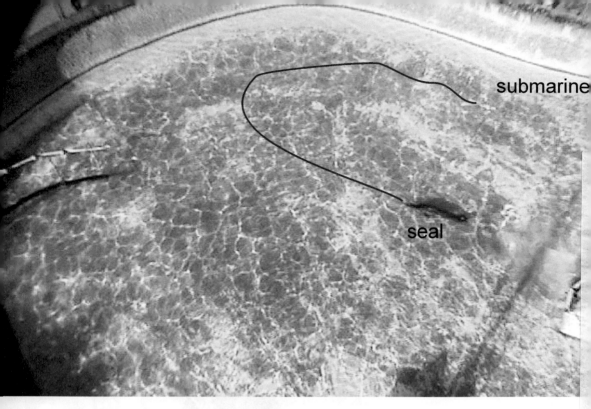

Top view of the pool where Henry follows the submarine. The red line traces the ripple trail left by the submarine (yellow). Henry will follow the trail and find the submarine even though he's blindfolded.

The ripple trail left by the toy submarine was similar to the trail left by swimming fish. So, the scientists thought, if Henry could follow the submarine's tracks, then he could probably follow a trail left by prey like fish.[5]

After Henry learned to find the submarine underwater, the next experiment was to find out if Henry could locate the submarine without being able to see or hear. To test this, the scientists covered Henry's ears with headphones and blindfolded him with a stocking mask before having him follow the submarine.[6]

Even though Henry could not see or hear the submarine, he found it as easily as when his eyes and ears were uncovered. The scientists decided to try to trick Henry by having the submarine suddenly change its course, just like a fish would do. Would Henry be able to follow a change of direction in the ripple trail? Henry showed the scientists that he could. When the submarine suddenly turned, Henry also turned onto the new course when he found the trail.

Do the Twist!

The scientists observed that when Henry was signaled to find the submarine, he immediately submerged and headed toward the center of the pool. Then, Henry protracted his whiskers, or moved them to the most forward position. Without moving the whiskers, Henry twisted his head slightly to the left and right.[7]

As soon as he detected the ripple trail, he turned into it and followed it exactly. The scientists observed this behavior using video recordings taken with a camera placed above the pool. Then, they watched the videos frame by frame. Henry found the submarine in 256 of 326 trials.[8] This is about 80 percent of the time, which is pretty good considering he cannot see or hear!

The scientists realized that Henry's whiskers might be helping him feel the ripple trail left by the submarine. But they needed direct proof of this. They asked more questions: What if Henry could not use his whiskers to feel the ripples?

Close up underwater view of Henry wearing a sock over his face. The whiskers are free to move, so even though he cannot see, his super sensitive whiskers will guide him to find the ripple trail.

Would he still be able to find the trail?

Clueless in the Water

To test this idea, the researchers covered Henry's muzzle with a stocking mask. The mask did not allow the water motion caused by the submarine to move the whiskers, but Henry was still able to open his mouth freely. Then the experiment began. The submarine propelled itself under the water, and Henry received the signal to go and find it.[9]

Henry started the search as before; he went under the water and twisted his head right and left. But this time the muzzle held his whiskers still. This prevented ripples from moving the whiskers and Henry could not feel the trail.[10]

Dr. Dehnhardt and his team had uncovered the harbor seal's secret. By projecting the whiskers fully forward, harbor seals can feel the itsy-bitsy movements of water stirred up by passing fish and then, rush upon them and gulp!

4
SPONGER MOMS

When it comes to finding food, dolphins living at Shark Bay, Australia, have at least eleven different ways of going about it. Only apes such as chimpanzees and orangutans seem to also have such a variety of hunting tactics. Dolphins and apes are the highest-ranking animals in intelligence.

One of the dolphin's hunting strategies is to probe or explore the ocean floor with its snout. This is a successful hunting strategy. However, some dolphins at Shark Bay seem to have come up with an improvement.

What Is That Bump?
The first clue that some dolphins had developed a new hunting strategy came about twenty years

Bottlenose dolphins can reach three to four meters in length (ten to thirteen feet). The Shark Bay dolphins tend to average about two meters (seven feet) long.[1]

On average, they weigh about two hundred kilograms (four hundred forty pounds). A small pony weighs about 225 kg (five hundred pounds). Shark Bay dolphins probably weigh much less—about one hundred kilograms (two hundred twenty pounds).

Besides fish, dolphins also like to eat squid and cuttlefish and will occasionally eat rays. On two occasions, the researchers at Shark Bay saw an old male eat a small shark!

Dolphins swallow fish whole, headfirst. They do not use their teeth to chew. If they have a large fish, they may use their beak to break the fish on the bottom of the seafloor. When they do this, they often do not eat the head of the fish.

ago. A boater watching the dolphins noticed that one of them had something bumpy on its snout. At first, the boater thought it was a tumor. A tumor is an abnormal growth of tissue in the body that may feel and look like a bump. But after watching more closely, it was clear that it was not a bump. The dolphin actually had a sea sponge on its snout.[2]

The scientists were curious. Why was this dolphin carrying a sponge on its snout? They became even more curious when over the years they saw more dolphins carrying sea sponges on their snouts. In the Shark Bay population, about 15 out of 141 dolphins have been observed wearing a sponge. What could this trend mean?

Like a Glove

After many observations, the marine biologists concluded that dolphins seem to use the sponge as a tool. A sponger dolphin breaks a marine sponge off the seafloor and wears it over its snout like people wear gloves on their hands. Then, the dolphin scrapes and probes the ocean floor

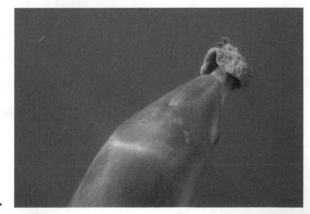

Dodger the dolphin carries a marine sponge covering most of his snout to protect it from scratches when he searches for a meal.

many times with its sponge-covered snout searching for fish. Scientists called this strategy "sponging."[3]

Dr. Michael Krützen from Switzerland and his team of American, Australian, and Canadian scientists have been observing spongers for many years. They have found out that

sponger dolphins usually work alone for a long time poking the seafloor with their sponge-covered snout.

The scientists think that sponging protects dolphins from being stung by dangerous fish like stonefish that may be hiding on the ocean floor. The stonefish has highly venomous spikes, and wearing a marine sponge on the snout may shield spongers from receiving a deadly sting. The sponge also seems to disturb the fish hiding in the sandy seabed. As soon as the fish dart out, the dolphin snaps them up![4]

Dolphins in captivity, like nineteen-year-old Boris here, may not need to use a snout sponge to find their daily meals.

A dolphin uses a sponge to search for food on the sandy and scratchy ocean floor.

From Mother to Daughter

As Dr. Krützen and his team continued studying sponger dolphins, they discovered that a dolphin is not born knowing how to sponge. The scientists at Shark Bay have seen dolphin moms sponging while their daughters were watching and imitating mom's behavior. These observations have led the scientists to conclude that sponger moms seem to show sponging to their daughters.

It turned out that not all dolphins in Shark Bay practice sponging. One of the most intriguing things about it is that almost all spongers are females. Only one out of thirteen spongers studied was a male.[5]

It is still a mystery why male dolphins do not practice sponging as much as females do. The scientists have observed that both sons and daughters spend about the same time with their mothers during their growing years. But even though both seem to have the same chance to learn sponging, only daughters become spongers. It seems that sponging is like a mother-and-daughter tradition.

The secret is out. Dolphins can make and use tools. Sponging dolphins were unheard of before. Only people, chimps, orangutans, and crows were thought to be capable of making and using tools to make their lives easier.[6] Now dolphins have joined the list and made scientists wonder: What else do we not know?

5
BUBBLE TRICK

t is not easy being a wild Weddell seal. Just ask Ally McSeal and other Weddell seals living at McMurdo Station in Antarctica. Ally spends her days and nights in the coldest place on Earth. It gets so cold that even her whiskers get covered in icicles!

Ally swims in ice-cold seawater and must catch lots of fast-moving fish to stay alive. Borks are one of her favorite fish. These small fish are not only fast swimmers but also have learned to hide to prevent Weddell seals from turning them into lunch. Borks hide in crevices or cracks on ice sheets that form at the surface of the sea.[1] They are not an easy meal to find. However, Ally and other Weddell seals have many tricks that allow them to succeed on their hunting trips.

Many of the seals' hunting strategies, however, have remained secret to marine biologists. The main reason is that studying deep-diving mammals living in the freezing waters of Antarctica is not an easy task. Although this is so, scientists from Texas and California have figured out ways to take a peek at the secret underwater world of Weddell seals.

> **Science Tongue Twisters:**
> *The scientific name of Ally McSeal the Weddell seal is* **Leptonychotes weddellii.**
> *Bork fish are called* **Pagothenia borchgrevinki.**

Camera, Action!

No film crew would dare accompany Weddell seals on their hunting trips. So, Dr. Randall W. Davis at Texas A&M University in Galveston and his colleagues thought that if they could not go with the seals, then they would have the seals record their explorations and bring them back.

> **Meet the Scientists:**
> *Dr. Randall W. Davis and his colleagues are marine biologists interested in understanding how aquatic mammals behave underwater.*

To do this, they needed to design instruments small enough for a seal to carry easily. The instruments also needed to be able to work well in spite of the very cold temperatures and the pressure applied by the deep. Weddell seals may dive as deep as four hundred meters (1,312 feet) or more. Of course, the instruments had to be sealed in a waterproof case. The scientists did not want the seals to be distracted by the lights

A Weddell seal scratches an itch while relaxing near McMurdo Sound in the Antarctic.

of the camera, so they used near-infrared light, which seals cannot see.[2]

It took Dr. Davis and his team years, but they came up with a set of electronic gadgets that were capable of filming what seals do in freezing, deep seawater. The gadgets did more than filming. They also recorded sounds made by the seals and their prey, as well as the seals' location, the direction they swim, depth, speed, and how many times the seals stroke their tails.[3]

The camera was small enough to fit on top of a seal's head. The camera was connected with a short cable to the rest of the gadgets placed on the seal's back. The whole set of gadgets was inside a case that looked like a small torpedo. It was about as long as a laptop computer and as thick as a medium grapefruit. All this equipment allowed the scientists to have "front-row seats" to observe the Weddell seals' under-water show.[4]

The Seal Hole

Once Dr. Davis and his team had the equipment ready to go, they thought about a very important question. How could they make sure that they would get it back from the seal? The scientists knew that diving seals always come back to the surface to breathe and that would be the perfect time to

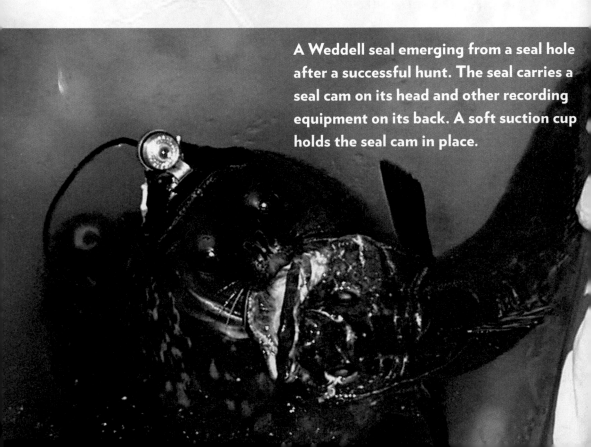

A Weddell seal emerging from a seal hole after a successful hunt. The seal carries a seal cam on its head and other recording equipment on its back. A soft suction cup holds the seal cam in place.

recover the gear. But, how could they know where the seal would surface? They decided to mark the spot for the seals.

The scientists made a seal hole, or a deep hole in the ice in a large area of solid ice. It would be the only hole in the area the seal could use to surface to breathe. Then they captured a seal, geared it up with the camera and the torpedo-shaped case, and let it dive into the dark, freezing seawater. Now, they just had to wait for the seal to come back, and they could recover the equipment and discover the seals' deep-water secrets.[5]

Flush It Out!

Ally McSeal and other Weddell seals brought back the first glimpses of their secret underwater life that no scientist had ever seen before. Some of the recordings showed a trick seals

A bork (below) is one of the Weddell seals' favorite meals.

★ Besides eating lots of bork, Weddell seals also like feasting on cod, silverfish, squid, shrimp, and krill. Cod are large fish of about one hundred sixty-five centimeters (sixty-five inches) long and weigh about eighty kilograms (one hundred seventy-five pounds). But silverfish are much smaller than cod, just about the size of an anchovy, or about eight centimeters (three inches) long. One cod may make one meal, but seals need many silverfish to satisfy their appetite. In one single dive, Ally McSeal gulped about a hundred silverfish![6]

★ Weddell seals are very large animals. The seals that worked with the scientists in these experiments weighed about four hundred seventy kilograms (one thousand thirty pounds)![7]

★ Dr. Davis and his colleagues have a radio transmitter and a satellite tag attached to the seal gear to help them know where the seal is. They keep working at improving their equipment. For example, they are making it smaller so it is even easier for the seals to carry it.[8]

A "seal-cam" placed on top of this Weddell seal's head records the hunter's bubble trick. The photo on the top (A) shows the seal blowing bubbles out of its nostrils into a crevice in the underwater sea ice where "bork" fish are hiding. See the seals forehead, muzzle, and vibrissae (whiskers). The bottom photo (B) shows a fish coming out of the crevice after the seal has successfully played her bubble trick.

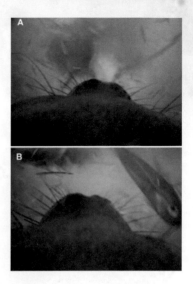

use to hunt under "platelet ice." This ice is made of large, loosely compacted crystals and can be more than one meter (3.3 feet) thick. This is the place where bork fish hide inside cracks to avoid being eaten.

The video recordings showed that the seal first swam under the ice using its eyes to scan the surface from beneath. This exploration allowed the seal to see if there was a fish hiding in the ice. If there was, most likely the seal would see the fish's shape against the light on the surface. This is called "backlighting," and seals and other aquatic animals use it to hunt their prey.[9]

After scanning the surface, the seal slowly ascended toward the ice. Suddenly, the seal lunged from one side to the other five times. It seemed like it had seen something. The recording on the seal's head showed a small fish darting under the ice.

The seal ascended more, getting just a few centimeters from the ice where two bork fish could be seen in a crevice. Then the seal did the trick. The seal blew a blast of air through its nostrils for one second and one of the fish immediately swam out of the crevice. This bork was lucky. The seal tried to catch it, but she failed and returned to the ice looking for the remaining fish.[10]

During another dive, the seal again blew air into the ice from beneath and then plunged its head into the soft ice three times for four to six seconds at a time. Right after she backed up from the ice the third time, the seal jerked its head to either side three times, just like a dog chewing on something hard would do. This time, the seal had gotten its reward![11]

Dr. Davis and his colleagues were the first ones to see Weddell seals perform the bubble trick. They were amazed at how seals play with different hunting strategies to get their meals. From backlighting to flushing fish out of their hiding, seals have many ways to get a meal and survive in the coldest place on Earth.

★ CHAPTER NOTES ★

Chapter 1. Diving Dolphin's Secret

1. Terrie M. Williams, et al., "Sink or Swim: Strategies for Cost-efficient Diving by Marine Mammals," *Science*, Vol. 288, April 7, 2000, pp. 133–136.
2. Tim Stephens, "Video Cameras Reveal Marine Mammals Take a Laid-back Approach to Deep Diving," University of California Santa Cruz, *Currents online*, April 10, 2000, <http://www.ucsc.edu/currents/99-00/04-10/dive.html> (September 11, 2007).
3. Williams, et al., p.134.
4. E-mail interview with Dr. Terrie Williams, October 17, 2001.
5. Ibid.
6. Gerald L. Kooyman and P. J. Ponganis, "The Challenges of Diving to Depth," course material at University of California, Santa Cruz.
7. Williams, et al., p. 134.
8. Ibid.
9. Ibid.
10. Kooyman and Ponganis.
11. Kooyman and Ponganis, Figure 2.
12. Peter L. Tyack, et al., "Extreme Diving of Beaked Whales," *The Journal of Experimental Biology*, Vol. 209, 2006, pp. 4238–4253.

Chapter 2. Sleepless in the Ocean

1. Jerome M. Siegel, "Why We Sleep. The Reasons That We Sleep Are Gradually Becoming Less Enigmatic," *Scientific American*, November 2003, p. 96.
2. Oleg Lyamin, et al., "Continuous Activity in Cetaceans After Birth," *Nature*, Vol. 435, June 30, 2005, p. 1177.

3. Ibid.

4. Jerome M. Siegel, "Clues to the Functions of Mammalian Sleep," *Nature*, Vol. 437, October 27, 2005, p. 1264–1271.

5. Oleg Lyamin, et al., p. 1177.

6. Siegel, "Why We Sleep," pp. 92–97.

7. E-mail interview with Dr. Jerome Siegel, November 28, 2006.

Chapter 3. Hungry Seals Do the Twist

1. Guido Dehnhardt and A. Kaminski, "Sensitivity of the Mystacial Vibrissae of Harbor Seals (Phoca vitulina) for Size Differences of Actively Touched Objects," *The Journal of Experimental Biology*, Vol. 198, 1995, pp. 2317–2323.

2. E-mail interview with Dr. Guido Dehnhardt, November 15, 2006.

3. Dehnhardt and Kaminski, p. 2322.

4. Ibid, p. 2317

5. Guido Dehnhardt, et al., "Seal Whiskers Detect Water Movements," *Nature*, Vol. 394, July 16, 1998, pp. 235–236.

6. Guido Dehnhardt, et al., "Hydrodynamic Trail-following in Harbor Seals (Phoca vitulina)," *Science*, Vol. 293, July 6, 2001, pp. 102–104.

7. Ibid., p. 103.

8. Ibid.

9. Ibid.

10. Ibid.

Chapter 4. Sponger Moms

1. "Dolphin Q&A," Monkey Mia Research Foundation, <http://www.monkeymiadolphins.org/> (September 11, 2007).

2. Michael Krützen, et al., "Cultural Transmission of Tool Use in Bottlenose Dolphins," *Proceedings of the National Academy of Sciences, USA*, Vol. 102, June 21 2005, pp. 8939–8943.

3. Georgetown University, Office of Communications, "New Research Examines Dolphins Feeding Habits," July 7, 2005,

<http://explore.georgetown.edu/news/?ID=2475> (September 11, 2007).

4. James Owen, "Dolphin Moms Teach Daughters to Use Tools," *National Geographic News*, June 7, 2005, <http://news.nationalgeograph ic.com/news/2005/06/0607_050607_dolphin_tools.html> (September 11, 2007).

5. Krützen, et al., p. 8941.

6. Krützen, et al., p. 8939.

Chapter 5. Bubble Trick

1. Terrie M. Williams, "Antarctic Expedition, The Foraging Biology of Weddell Seals," 2001, <http://bio.research.ucsc.edu/people/williams/antarctic/index. html> (September 11, 2007).

2. Randall W. Davis, et al., "Hunting Behavior of a Marine Mammal Beneath the Antarctic Fast Ice," *Science*, Vol. 283, February 12, 1999, pp. 993–996.

3. Randall W. Davis, et al., "Monitoring the Behavior and Multi-dimensional Movements of Weddell Seals Using Animal-borne Video and Data Recorder," *Mem. National Institute of Polar Research*, Spec. Issue # 58, 2004, pp. 150–156.

4. Ibid., p. 151.

5. Williams.

6. Davis, et al., "Hunting Behavior of a Marine Mammal Beneath the Antarctic Fast Ice," p. 993.

7. Williams.

8. Davis, et al., "Monitoring the Behavior and Multi-dimensional Movements of Weddell Seals Using Animal-borne Video and Data Recorder," p.155.

9. Williams.

10. Davis, et al., "Hunting Behavior of a Marine Mammal Beneath the Antarctic Fast Ice," p. 994.

11. Ibid.

★ GLOSSARY ★

aquatic ★ Living in water.

behavior ★ The way somebody or something acts.

blubber ★ A thick layer of fat under the skin of aquatic mammals.

echolocation ★ To locate an object using sound and the reflection back from it.

gestation period ★ The time it takes for a new baby to develop in its mother's womb.

glide ★ To move in a smooth, effortless way.

hertz ★ A measurement of how many times a periodic event takes place; one hertz indicates the event happens once every second. For sound, the higher the hertz, the higher the frequency or pitch.

hydrodynamic ★ Moved by a liquid.

insulator ★ A material that prevents or reduces the passage of heat.

mammal ★ A warm-blooded animal that produces milk to feed its young.

marine ★ Of the sea.

nerve ★ A bundle of fibers that transmits messages between the brain and the body.

predator ★ An animal that hunts, kills, and eats other animals to survive.

probe ★ An instrument used to explore or examine.

saddle ★ A seat used by a rider on the back of an animal such as a horse.

seabed ★ The floor of the ocean.

terrestrial ★ Living on land.

vibrissae ★ Animal whiskers that vibrate when touched.

★ FURTHER READING ★

Books

Hirschmann, Kris. *Creatures of the Sea—Killer Whales.* Detroit, Mich., KidHaven Press, 2005.

Taylor, Leighton R. *Dolphins.* Minneapolis, Minn., Lerner Publishers, 1999.

Weider, Kathleen Zoenfeld. *Seal Pup Grows Up: The Story of a Harbor Seal.* Norwalk, Conn., Smithsonian Oceanic Collection, Sound Prints, 1994.

Williams, Terrie M. *The Hunter's Breath: On Expedition with the Weddell Seals of the Antarctic.* New York, N.Y., M. Evans and Company, Inc., 2004.

Internet Addresses

Ana María Rodríguez's Homepage

> http://www.anamariarodriguez.com

The Mammalian Physiology Lab at UCSC

> http://bio.research.ucsc.edu/people/williams/

Marine Science Center

> http://www.marine-science-center.de/centerE.htm

The Department of Marine Biology, Texas A&M University at Galveston

> http://www.marinebiology.edu/links.htm

★ INDEX ★